VIA Folios 106

Perhaps Fly

Selected Poems by
ALBERT TACCONELLI

Bordighera Press

Library of Congress Control Number: 2014947177

Printed in the United States.

Published by
Bordighera Press
John D. Calandra Italian American Institute
25 West 43rd Street, 17th Floor
New York NY 10036

VIA Folios 106
ISBN 978-1-59954-068-9

Special thanks to the editors of the following publications in which these poems, some in earlier versions, first appeared:

"Two Comari Marys," *Paterson Literary Review*, 2013
"Seahorse," *Philadelphia Poets*, 2011
"Perhaps Fly," *Philadelphia Poets*, 2011
"Sooner or Later," *Philadelphia Poets*, 2011
"All Saints Eve," *Philadelphia Poets*, 2011
"Listening," *Philadelphia Poets*, 2009
"Our Porch," *Philadelphia Poets*, 2009
"Compare Henry, Comare Mary, and Junior," *Philadelphia Poets*, 2007
"My Father, Gladioli," *Philadelphia Poets*, 2004
"Wine Cellar," *VIA*, 2005
"As I Raked And Swept," *VIA*, 2005

"Big Joe" first appeared in the chapbook, *Short Stack*, 2008

Poems listed below have been awarded:

 "The Blessing," Editor's Choice, Allen Ginsberg Poetry Awards, 2009
"Saint Joseph's Day Eggs," Editor's Choice, Allen Ginsberg Poetry Awards, 2008
"Nonna's Rosaries," Editor's Choice, Allen Ginsberg Poetry Awards, 2007

*For my parents who have given me
everything that is good, and my ancestors
whose blood is my life.*

*Beloved dead, some of these poems
would not have pleased you,
but in heaven such is inconsequential.*

My gratitude to
Maria Famà and Mary Russo Demetrick
For their friendship, inspiration, and insight.

CONTENTS

UNALTERABLE

CHILDHOOD BREAKFAST

No concerns about cholesterol, every morning
Ma beat one egg, sugar, McCormick's pure vanilla
extract into a sweet frothy yellow eggnog.

I remember Sacchetti's Italian bread sliced, toasted,
spread thick with Land o' Lakes butter, dunked
into hot coffee with sugar and lots of milk.

Each morning this simple breakfast Ma prepared
—her son's sustenance for the years ahead.

CLOUDS

Little boy in overalls stood on corner,
Haverford & County Line, hands in pockets,
head upturned, awed by spectacular
early Sunday morning sky.

Southwest to northeast, cirrocumulus clouds
marched majestically above huge silver maples,
sagging stone wall, old half-hidden
English Tudor-style house owned by the Farrs,
above his house—parents, grandparents,
older brothers, different clouds.

TEDDY BEAR

Decades have disappeared, like
my floppy brown teddy bear
with big yellow glass eyes.
Every night I took my teddy
bear to bed; in the morning
when I woke it was gone.
Soon as I fell asleep Ma eased
the teddy bear from my arms.
So you won't suffocate, Ma said.
If while sleeping I suffocated
what would have happened?
Was there heaven for a sad
little boy and his teddy bear?

SPECIAL SUMMER

Six years old in the summer of '44. Why was
I sent to stay with Aunt Loretta, Uncle Lawrence,
cousins Rachel, Rita, Roy, and Vincent—modest
duplex on North Sycamore, quiet side street,
quiet neighborhood in blue-collar Clifton Heights?

Gray-white gravel from the quarry Uncle Lawrence
labored forty backbreaking years crunched beneath
my feet on the driveway leading to the garage,
and to immaculate wire mesh coops housing
clucking brown and white, egg-laying hens.

House, garage, everything—spotless white,
trimmed shiny "park bench" green. Saturday
afternoon, big brushes dripping like vanilla
ice cream, Uncle Lawrence and I carefully
white washed the driveway's low stone wall.

Special summer of '44 living with loving Rachel
and Rita—rough, yet caring Roy and Vincent
—Aunt Loretta, who resembled Da Vinci's
"Lady with an Ermine"—and Uncle Lawrence,
mirror image of Pope John XXIII.

Labor Day weekend, last days of summer,
last days being youngest of four siblings.
When I returned home Johnny waited,
new baby brother—it was then I knew why.

UNALTERABLE

In the cool dark garage next to our house, I escaped
family chaos rummaging dusty clutter, exploring
things forgotten, or abandoned like Bill the butcher's
red-enameled Rube Goldbergesque meat grinding machine
from Uncle Theodore's unsuccessful grocery store.

Beneath Tommy's battered pale green bicycle,
stashed in a junk filled cardboard box, I found what
I'd never seen, what tough older guys called a 2X4,
small cartoon booklet—provocative drawings
of men and women in pornographic contortions.
Carefully I hid the surprise find since like FBI
and Scotland Yard, nothing escaped Ma's eagle eyes.

Sunday afternoon I met another kid also searching
Haverford College pond to catch wild goldfish.
Hidden among shrubs we imitated 2X4 cartoons.
Overwhelmed later with Catholic guilt, I
headed home & bathed thoroughly, but that
afternoon, no matter how thorough the bathing,
something unalterable happened—I'd become
an adolescent fumbling towards manhood.

THE OLD CUSTOM

I CHOOSE

I choose to remain silent.
Santa Pacienza presses
a peasant's aged finger
against my lips—Nonna's.

NONNA'S ROSARIES

Rosaries, endless recitation of rosaries,
earnest prayers for whom, for what—
were they answered ever?

From one of your broken rosaries I kept
a small tarnished silver crucifix, its corpus
worn smooth from fingered prayers.

Perhaps they were answered, was it
countless rosaries that protected
me in my yet unfurled future?

As a child, to your gratitude's amazement,
I threaded needles mending rips
and holes in hand-me-down clothes.

Dear Nonna, we are becoming forgotten.
Soon I must bid farewell to loves whose
loveliness is my undoing—will your

faithful rosaries guide me across eternity
to be with those who've rejected me, will
my shameful follies be at last forgiven?

ST. JOSEPH'S DAY EGGS

1.

Today is St. Joseph's feast day, but I didn't go
to Mass to celebrate the family's and laborer's
patron saint, whose holy card my father
kept in the cash register at his work place—
to bless and provide. St. Joseph, to whom
for years I prayed not to lose my job.

2.

I remember our small kitchen, Ma's big
aluminum pot filled with spicy tomato sauce.
How Nonna cracked open eggs, dropped them
into simmering sauce—poached they
looked like plump, tomato encrusted oysters,
eggs that tasted so good. Not scrambled,

or fried, no frittata, but St. Joseph's day eggs
poached in my mother's tomato sauce. I
tried to do the same—disaster, not even close,
nothing how Nonna's looked or tasted.
St. Joseph's feast. Today I remember Nonna's
specially prepared tomato poached eggs.

NONNA'S ADMONITION

I remember that day in the kitchen,
Nonna's withered hands—knuckles
swollen, blue veins bulging, coursing
through arid, brown-splotched terrain.

From across the small wooden table
Nonna pointed, touched my left hand,
said solemnly, "Never forget,
in your veins flows Italian blood."

ALL SAINTS EVE

Last night the month of holy angels
became the month of dead remembered,
    souls gone yet present.

After supper Nonna used to set
on clean table cloth bottles of
my father's wine, olive oil,
fresh loaves of bread covered
with big white napkins—
    for the dead to bless.

At midnight, Nonna said, among
the bottles and loaves they hovered,
until wine, olive oil, bread
commingled with remembered dead—
what once sustained them,
    blessed to nourish us.

NONNO'S BAKED POTATOES

Basement of my father's workplace.
Nonno showed me how to bury potatoes
under glowing embers in the old coal furnace.
Lunch time my task was to carry home a
small basket Nonno filled with baked potatoes.
Removing remaining ashes, Ma
mashed them, skins and all, on a large
serving platter. Sprinkled with *Pace Mio Dio* oil,
salt, a few red flakes of dried hot pepper—
fragrance like church incense rising.

THE OLD CUSTOM

Last morning, your casket's lid was closed in the
flower-filled living room of our house—old country
within new country, where you, wise patriarch,
wielded absolute authority over everyone,

even your son's sons. My parents once bought a
GE refrigerator, lied about its cost not to
provoke your Vesuvian Italian epithets.

Stroke-stricken grandfather, your love would have
paid for everything if I'd become a priest—I instead,
seminarian of lusty pagan gods, paid dearly.

Nonno, who will put a penny in my pocket as
Nonna did for you—Charon's price to ferry you
across dark, unruffled waters of everlasting;

who now would know the old custom,
in my pocket one penny for Charon's barque—
my reluctant crossing into eternity?

SOONER OR LATER

I ALWAYS KNEW

I always knew my mother was a saint,
certainly when Ma told me of a hungry
old homeless man who knocked at the kitchen door.
Ma invited him in to sit at the small
wooden table with its two blue chairs.
Gratefully he ate the sandwich Ma prepared.
He was a good man, my mother said,
because in his coat pocket he kept a rosary.

I NEVER SAW MY MOTHER WRITE

I never saw my mother write except to scrawl carefully,
letter by letter, her signature on my report card.
If Ma could, what would she have written.
Notes perhaps, hidden in the pantry under the sugar jar.

"I miss my mother, I miss my sister and brothers
three hours drive away, the world's other side,
here, chaotic family filled with arguments—
the dinner table a battle field.

Alone in this narrow kitchen, I cry for husband
brutalized by his family, and us, together brutalized.

Like a servant I am treated, for servant is what I am,
to his mother, father until he died, to loving sons—
whose selfishness hurts beyond pain.

On a thorny bed of my own making I lie. Migraines
betray body's undoing, heart deteriorated,
years of high blood pressure uncontrolled.

Between duty and death I waver, unending maternal
caring trying to help. For tragedy there is no help,
not even many rosaries.

Flowers on the porch look beautiful in pots brightly
        glazed,
and red rambling roses. In the garden I linger beneath
three honest fig trees, among leafy tomatoes—little
moments, the unhappiness I will not claim forgotten."

FUTILITY

> *. . . you took deadly risks daily*
> *to escape, to enter the good life*
> *that always glittered somewhere*
> *down the road, they didn't know*
> *about it, or didn't care to know.*
> —Thomas Centolella

Futile desperation lashed her
eldest son's shirtless back—each
strike of the strap her flesh stung deep.

Old world father rebellious son's
wayward life chastised—who,
from concrete cellar floor rose
unscathed, indifferent.

She pondered her early marriage,
unhappy family history,
chastisement's futility.

WHAT MA HEARD

Early June mornings, each day longer,
brighter, anticipating summer solstice.
Scattered with crinkled paint tubes,
water bowl, motley brushes, I enjoy sitting
at the small wood table painting and sipping
coffee from Carl Engstram's klutzy ceramic mug.
One, then two, later three beige-mauve
mourning doves maneuver themselves
up and down with cautious side steps on
the roof above Stephanie Matkov's deck.
I hear their plaintiff cooing: ooo-woo-woo-woo,
ooo-woo-woo-woo—silence, then
ooo-woo-woo-woo, ooo-woo-woo-woo.
I remember Ma also looking out the kitchen
window listening to those shy feathered
mourners, comment how sad their song.
What did Ma hear, was it ooo-woo-woo-woo
or oh-woe-woe-woe-is-me. I wonder.

MAY'S FIRST ROSES

Unhappy spring, chronic condition
required another of Ma's infrequent
but serious hospitalizations.
After supper before his nightly visit,

Ba stood tiptoe beneath the rose
wreathed trellis, with scissors
searched lush leaves, snipped
a fistful of blooming red ramblers.

I remember Ba's thoughtful gesture,
devoted husband's heartfelt,
waxpaper wrapped gift—May's first
roses for Ma already dying.

FASTIDIOUS RELIGIOSITY

Fastidious religiosity unclasped
your hand's firm grip, fingers
clinging around my forearm.

Intensive Care to evening Mass
I went—futile prayers for my
dying mother's recovery.

Why didn't I understand
dying mother, powerless son
    were Mass.

MA'S SPRING

Miraculously discharged from the hospital
well enough to come home,
we refused to believe you were dying;
your long gray coat hung loosely.

I can't wait until it's warm, you said,
to plant flowers in the soil again.
Spring arrived early with Easter—no
flowers, in the cold earth we planted you.

FAMILY TIMES SIX

1.

They arrived at last; Aunt Virginia, Aunt Dottie, Uncle Paul,
Uncle Jack, Aunt Eva—to see you, with pillows propped,
long black hair always neatly combed, arranged
by nurses in tidy disarray—to hear their dying
sister's barely audible, "Why did it take you so long."

2.

Day and night Holy Week, your passion week,
we took bedside turns. At home, Aunt Dottie's cigarette
smoke filled the house, coffee pot perked, around
the kitchen table family comforted each other.

3.

I wanted to go with Joseph, Johnny, and Uncle Jack.
"Hospital room too crowded. Tomorrow."
"What if there isn't tomorrow," I questioned.
Uncle Jack's eyes understood, but said nothing.

4.

Early Holy Saturday morning front door opened.
I could hear Joseph gently say to Ba, "Mother is gone."
Aunts, uncles wept, and for your years absent
from Poughkeepsie, where, though never spoken,
they believed you would have had a happier life.

5.

Dripping melting ice on your parched tongue ceased.
Johnny said he understood for the first time,
"rest in peace" because after you died, profound
tranquility permeated the room's silence.

6.

For grieving father and brothers, for my aunts
and uncles, you were the life taken from their lives.
I was severed from the world forever.

SOONER OR LATER

Sooner or later it had to be done, empty closets
and dresser of your clothing—strange
feeling, as if you were being violated,
    so palpable your presence.

I found a Christmas present I'd given how
many Christmases ago—white dressing
gown with small pink rosebuds still
in its special gift box, still neatly folded,
    waiting for some better day.

Closets and dresser were emptied, clothing
donated or given away. The house too,
of its life had been emptied,
    gone was our better day.

CRUEL WORDS

Rosaries, blessed palms, red votive glass,
Compare Henry's 1950 Vatican Jubilee Year memento,
painted plaster saints old as Nonna, disappeared
the day relatives took Nonna to live with them.
Why didn't they believe Ma's grave illness,
and Ma months from dying.

Wearing long-sleeved electric blue dress,
Ma lay cold at Stretch Funeral Home,
long sleeves concealing unsightly IV bruises
makeup and powder could not conceal.
Aunts, uncles, cousins grieved too late,
too many cruel words hurled like knives
wounded Ma already pale with death.

MA'S DREAM

I rose without waking your father,
from bedroom window I saw hovering
above the Farrs' huge silver maples, a
long table draped with white table cloth,
overflowing with steaming platters and
casseroles—as if for a holiday.
Slowly traversing the night sky
the festal table floated left to right,
north to south until lost from sight.

Ma's mysterious dream eluded us.
Years now, I believe Ma was the table.
While without gratitude we sated ourselves,
imperceptibly the table disintegrated,
light and life to darkness and death.

AS I RAKED AND SWEPT

The mystery is we suffer
without deliverance,
and love suffers what's real.
          —W. S. Piero

Under shedding holly tree I raked,
along neglected curb I swept.

Slowly, imperceptibly,
every unkind word, love rejected,
opportunity squandered,
squeezed tight my dry throat.

I remembered you, Ma, doing chores,
thankless, taken for granted,
times you were especially silent—
     unspoken unhappiness.

In a bed of sorrows you slept;
migraines, high blood pressure,
lastly, enlarged heart stopped beating.
     Death, I pray,
disclosed a happier place—
we didn't know how to love you.

SILENTLY BEHIND

It would happen Saturday evenings, kitchen door
burst open, nonstop boisterous onslaught.
Ma's family came to visit—Grandma's sad eyes
ringed with dark circles; Aunt Virginia's still
in vogue forties style hairdo, dress and shoes;
Uncle Jimmy's staccato speech, slicked-back hair,
classic Sicilian profile; Angela's and Maryjane's comic
New York accents. Uncle Tony never visited,
phobia crossing bridges. Jazz saxophonist, Little Joe,
chauffeured Uncle Tony's shiny black Cadillac.

Ba's usual reserve, Ma's learned reserve,
laughed as everybody around kitchen table
joked and bantered the latest spicy gossip. No
matter how late, no one wanted to go to bed.
First to turn in, first to rise, Uncle Jimmy,
anxious for the long drive back to Poughkeepsie.
But not before huge Sunday dinner—spaghetti,
which Uncle Jimmy said he could eat for breakfast,
bowls of pasta, meatballs, bracioli, hot and sweet
sausage, salad, fruit, Ba's homemade red wine.

Chatter died down after dinner, inevitable parting,
unspoken, their sadness not taking Ma.
Tearful final embraces, all piled into Uncle Tony's
waiting Cadillac—three hour return to their world,
while Ma remained silently behind in her world.

FAMILY PHOTOS

There's no reason for the family's few photos.
Only important occasions like baptisms,
first holy communions, confirmations,
high school graduations. Some photos
Johnny and I took as we grew older survived.
Not surprising, Ma's rare photos are
treasured relics of our life-giving saint.

Alas, photos preserve irrevocable losses.
Ma died eight o'clock Holy Saturday morning.
Ba and Ma's family chatted at breakfast around
dining room table. From the den I heard
front door open. Joseph, Johnny, Uncle Jack.
Joseph said gently to Ba, Mother is gone—
everyone wept and sobbed.

I wanted to be with Ma at the hospital,
but Uncle Jack said, Tomorrow. I said, what if . . .
The very moment was what if—nothing
could bring Ma back alive and well again;
who can raise the dead with words.*
I felt suspended above an immense abyss
forever severed from the world,
into that vast void I fell headlong.

*Aeschylus, *Agamemnon*

PERHAPS FLY

I NEVER KNEW

I never really knew my father, though I've tried
to piece together a series of remembered episodes.
Some pleasant, some unpleasant

remain of him whom we called "Ba,"
short for Ba-Ba, the Abruzzese word for father.
Perhaps Ba didn't know who he was.

"You don't understand," Ba once said,
"they used my skin *come sporca mappine*."
Yes, to wipe the shit of patriarchal oppression.

Youngest son treated like a slave. Elder
brother, Theodore, wielded power. Ba obeyed.
Yet still a child, Ba's spirit withered.

Behind sudden outbursts, unpredictable rages,
Ba remained hidden. Obligation, or was it
love which drove my parents' unhappy years.

Who was my father, or my mother for that matter,
bound by marriage, actors together in a bad play,
final scene was death, first hers, lastly his.

EXPECTATION

Nothing unusual singing Christmas carols
around the piano at 924 County Line, Aunt Rose's
and Uncle Theodore 's home. At our house

we lived with unpredictable rage—seemed
my father was always angry. After high school
graduation ceremony Uncle Theodore
shook my hand. Ba gestured for mine,
but I withdrew my awkward hand.
Dear father, anger and frustration taught
five sons ridicule not affirmation.

NOTHING

Long hallway leading to the bedroom
five sons shared, out of nowhere
the unbuckled belt came down on us.
Terrified, Johnny and I cried,
"Why? We didn't do anything."

Impetuous rage crushed our spirit.
Nonno crushed Ba's spirit.
Generations of Abruzzese fathers
crushed their sons' spirit—submission,
domination, patriarchal oppression.

Abruptly the violence ended.
Life continued. Nothing changed.
Ba's brutality taught Johnny and me
we weren't sons, we were nothing,
nothing but shit in a family of shit.

LAYERS

Sometimes I've forgotten Ba's gentleness,
remember only the tyranny of rages.

One night after supper,
lying on living room floor, Ba explained
to me how an onion was formed. With
large sheet of manila paper and pencil,
with slow deliberate lines, each following
precisely the preceding line's contour,
an onion's tender interior appeared.

Like the onion, Ba's life a series of layers
concealing years of patriarchal oppression,
but that night, with an just ordinary pencil,
Ba drew his own unhurt heart deep within.

SEAHORSE

Late summers, I went with Ba and his friends deep
sea fishing to Tuckerton, Brigantine, Fortesque
for flounder, porgy, even mackerel. In Tuckerton,
Ba and I fished along the docks using his own hand-
made wire mesh nets in which we caught darting
schools of iridescent shiners—Ma later prepared,
then fried like fish n' chips.
                      Sometimes, while they
motored miles far off shore in crowded trollers—
I had fun on the docks lowering Ba's special mesh nets
anticipating what would surface. Once I caught a spiny
dark brown seahorse, around my finger it wrapped
its tail tightly as if afraid, away from its element.
Eventually, I let it go—into watery depths the
little seahorse disappeared, searching for home.

MY FATHER'S GLADIOLI

We used to plow them underfoot
scattering pink petals like curled tongues
over turned earth. Now they grow
in the garden tied with string,
undisturbed in their grace.

It was long ago. I was young.
It was another country.

LISTENING

There were Saturday nights, rare ones,
when I went out, usually Bridgeport,
to the old Lark Bar.
   In the den before I left,
I played Strauss's *Four Last Songs*
over and over. Elisabeth Schwartzkopf's
soaring soprano voice filled
the house, empty—except for
Ba in bed, not asleep. I sensed he too
listened to Strauss's lush melodies.

In retrospect, Ba knew why
I was listening to Strauss's music—
he knew me better than I thought.
   And tonight, listening
to the Four Last Songs, I realize
how much like Ba I am. They say,
the apple never falls far from the tree
—affable yet reserved, both of us
inhabiting an exclusive inner world.

Ba understood I sought music's
sublime solace to compensate
for the later scene's absurdity
—participating in a futile game,
didn't matter one way or
another if I met someone.
   Solitary in the Lark Bar,
noisy and crowded, I would be
consoled by art's transcendence—
Richard Strauss's *Four Last Songs*.

SIMILARITIES

Ba planted tomatoes in neat rows, afterwards
I gathered a handful of discarded sickly
seedlings left withering in the heat;
these I planted along the rusty wire fence
separating Ba's garden from our backyard.

Plenty of water, sun, loving care—tiny green
leaves on wilted seedlings soon appeared.
I imagined delicate yellow blossoms transformed
to lush tomatoes in salads Ma served with
Ba's red wine vinegar and *Pace Mio Dio* oil.

The day my rescued tomato plants vanished
taught me I didn't exist—without a word,
in his garden Ba replanted my tomato plants.
Since Ba never asked, ignored protests.
I learned I had no voice. I was nonentity.

Though Ba and I are much alike, I did not grow
up to be like the frail, stroke-stricken cripple
who managed to weave beautiful wicker baskets;
who survived eighteen solitary years without Ma.

PERHAPS FLY

To grasp and pull the church belltower rope,
above his shoulders Nonno hoisted his son
who rose and fell with the tolling
    bell's rhythmic momentum.

Nonno held tight for fear the little boy might
rise with the rope's ascent far beyond reach,
far beyond Abruzzo's ungentle mountains,
and glimpse Adriatic's limpid peripheries.

Decades later, that final dream, my father
saw himself soar free of those bound,
as his father had been bound—servile
centuries of patriarchal oppression.

LESS OF AN INSULT

I'd rather they didn't know that I knew,
Ba must have thought, lying there in their
bed half-empty—our recently dead mother.
We ignored years of Ma's symptoms.

In his own house Ba felt displaced by the
nursemaid employed at daughter-in-law's
insistence, son's compliance—a live-in
nursemaid no less—to make things easier
for Bebe, Joe's American wife, and little son, Joey.

Resigned, Ba bore the nursemaid's indignity.
At night, overhead in the attic where she slept,
Ba heard footsteps pacing to and fro, back and forth,
opening and closing closets and dresser drawers—
rummaging through Ma's hand stitched *biancheria*.

How many embroidered hand towels, pillowcases,
fine linen tablecloths were already missing.
Ba said nothing, less of an insult to remain silent.
Better they didn't know that at eight o'clock
Holy Saturday morning everything Ba loved died.

Was it fate or the stars, this old man's impotent
final years, to endure insults, outrages, humiliations?
Not one single word Ba uttered, while in his mind,
remaining still vividly alive, her memory,
their long life shared together—Ma forever gone.

ANTICIPATION

1.

Weekends home from Syracuse I made plans,
adjacent to living room windows I planted
several pyracantha shrubs. Thorny branches,
orange berry clusters deckled living room
windows, each glass pane a Hiroshige
color wood block print. I remember fall and
winter's limped light, how leafy violet
shadows shifted across pale stuccoed walls.
What grace, I thought, anticipating living
home again, transient past forgotten.

2.

Crippled by stroke, I remember Ba's patient,
hesitant shuffling from dining to living room.
Turandot's silent wizened emperor, Ba sat
on blue-cushioned chrome chair. I remember
emptiness, distance, the longing to embrace.

GUIDED TOUR, BREAKERS MANSION
for my father and Uncle Theodore

Which cornice, sconce, or rosy cherub
painted on ballroom ceiling high, did
your sweat, a day's wage of pennies buy?
Immigrant laborers' broken backs
Vanderbilt empire raised, gruel for
food, no *formaggio, pane, vino.*
Stifling stench, unbathed men, crowded
on narrow wooden pallets slept, and
I, on guided tour, marveled at wealth's
ostentatious display bought with sweat.

SUNDAY BEFORE CHRISTMAS 1985

Sunday, five a.m., the phone rang. Ba died.
My call woke Johnny. Nursing home's drab
hallways strung with plastic candy canes,
cheap Santa Claus cutouts led to Ba's room.
Startled at first, opening the door Johnny and
I didn't understand the window wide open,
December frigid through sheer curtains.
Sad, I thought, tiny wisp of a man
naked beneath crisp white cotton sheet
defenseless against the cold he shunned.
Overcome, Johnny fled the room leaving
Ba dead, and me, feeling like an orphan.
I was alone, an ethnic in exile.

MY FATHER SPEAKS TO ME

Above the yard's green wall of hedges neatly
trimmed, iridescent humming birds glinted.
I imagined flying among them free as when,
hoisted to Nonno's shoulders, I grasped and rose
with the church belltower's ascending rope.

Deceptive solitude—auto repair grime still
stains my creviced hands, grease clogs fingernails.
Remember when Ma taught me to walk again.
Summer evenings, remember us sitting here
Ma brushing and combing her long black hair.

Into back-breaking servitude I was born
while Nonna tended Abruzzo's sweat watered
furrows. *Come una sporca mappina* my flesh
wiped the shit of paternal oppression.

Would you have trusted *la via vecchia*,
had faith in your Baba's *contadino* wisdom
—learn patience, endure suffering.
You didn't trust. You didn't have faith.

But tell me, this brief past-present life,
is it one dream seamless and melancholy?
Losses say yes. Heart says no.
Neglected hedges grow higher.

RED SAUCE DESTINY

Sometimes from the Ninth Street Italian Market,
Ba returned with a big soggy brown paper
bag filled with wet caramel-yellow striped snails
crawling out—as quickly as Ma caught them.

Ma gave me a few snails to play with in the yard
—how effortlessly they slid over obstacles
I set, long antennae swaying back and forth.

Eventually my antennaed playmates joined
companions in Ma's old aluminum pot—
last attempts to escape red sauce destiny
served on a blue and white Woolworth platter.

Everyone raved at supper. I refused to eat
little snails I'd played with—such earnest
creatures who wanted only to be free.

AFTER THE FACT

WAS IT BY CHANCE
   for M. B.

Was it by chance that day as I drove down
Pennsylvania Avenue, rounded the curve near
the white stucco house your son, Tommy, would
not permit me to visit—in the driveway
I saw you sweeping leaves—you were always
sweeping or cleaning. I wanted Jasmine and Tyrone
to see their grandmother. I wanted to say
hello to the mother-in-law who taught me
to make tomato sauce, who taught me endurance,
who once confided she had shed tears
enough to wash all of Bryn Mawr.

And my own tears, for the abusive ex-husband
whose insanity barred me from Bryn Mawr Hospital
room as you lay dying the last weeks of Lent.

My decision to drive on I still regret.
Jasmine and Tyrone would have lifted your spirits.
Those few loving moments might have influenced
their lives for the better, saved Jasmine perhaps from
a pitifully young death from drugs—who knows.
I know their father's abuses made life hell.
Rest now, in the longed-for peace which came
neither to you nor to your broken family.

SUNDAY AFTERNOON EXCURSION

Sunday afternoon, no older brother driving
his kid brother for ice cream, or a matinee.
Tommy's flashy Olds headed for dreary
Conshohocken where dilapidated factories
clustered along polluted Schuylkill, and
blue-collar families lived hard lives—to

a dingy row house smoke filled kitchen.
Slippery sharks in soiled t-shirts crowded
the red formica table, intense sallow-faced
dealer dealt cards; piles of crumpled
bills were shoved from losers to winner,
who gambled winnings and lost,
gambled again, lost, then lost again.

Seemed like hours I stood invisible
among the gamblers—watching,
hating Tommy's tragic addiction.
Unhappy Tommy, unhappy family
crushed by incomprehensible ineptness.

AFTER THE FACT

I cried because life is hopeless and beautiful.
—Howard Nemerov

1.

Only a simple act of will was needed to get
my body moving from house to DCMH*,
see dying pathetic figment of my eldest brother,
Tommy, worn fragile as the rarest seashell
one harsh word could easily crush.

2.

Dying brother, I avoided the last chance
for grace perhaps to heal feelings too complex
to express. I did not want to face the final reality,
a life wasted, ridiculed, condemned by our
snickering, ever so saintly Catholic relatives.

I had planned to visit when Joseph drove
down from Montrose. Too late, you
were already dead when Joseph arrived.
What need was there to visit, since always
inside me the gash of your memory bleeds.

3.

Liberated by death from who you were,
eternally now who you truly are.
Your sad life's sad legacy—Joseph, Johnny
and me, burdened with unhappy memories.
And where is the healing of forgiveness.

*Delaware County Memorial Hospital

EASY TARGET

Easy target, Tommy was ridiculed,
shunned and hated; in Tommy's wake
trailed distressed and fractured lives.

Tommy always avoided responsibility,
finality's responsibility he could not avoid,
the petite body brooked no slippery words.

Death's decline came quickly—weak,
unconscious, shrunken to a whisper, frail
arms wire thin; prized gold Casio wristwatch

slipped hidden under Tommy's armpit, found
in the morgue by nurses among Tommy's sheets;
returned to faithful brother, Joseph.

Sad and tragic Uncle Tommy left nephew,
Ronny, a gold memento—parting gift
to another life broken, perhaps mending.

REMEMBERING LEWIS

1.

Animosity was your legacy bequeathed that day
in the backyard—spontaneous incomprehensible
hatred aimed, fired the BB gun, luckily
hitting only my thigh—from the kitchen
Aunt Loretta came running to see what happened.

Ashamed of where we lived you avoided staying home.
To look American like others guys on the wrestling
team you had yourself circumcised. Wearing
freshly ironed shirt you hung out at the Narberth Pub.

Small in stature, big ideas filled your head, big ideas
without perseverance. GMC Truck Dealership fiasco
        ruined
our family. No qualms forging checks for sweat-earned
        money.
Ba's reputation squashed bank officials legal action.
After creating chaos you headed west—old Chevy
loaded with belongings. We picked up the pieces.

Recently Joseph revealed he had been sexually abused.
Is this then the reason, my habitual acting out—that
forgotten or suppressed, you also abused me, ruthlessly
ridiculed target of guilt's projected self-loathing.

2.

Two special memories emerge from sadness—with
cousins Theresa and Maryann we saw Walt Disney's
        Bambi.
Children's eyes saw no animation, but a real live
Bambi fleeing real flaming forest. I cried hysterically.

We left, on your shoulders you carried me home still
    crying.

And second—while playing among piles of scrap wood
behind Ba's work place, the rusty nail you stomped on
to prevent me from harm, pierced the sole of your shoe.
Bryn Mawr Hospital gave you a tetanus shot.

3.

In San Francisco you succumbed to chronic stomach
    condition.
"After all," wept Johnny, "Lewis was our brother." I felt
    numb.
Never brothers, we could have tried to at least become
friends—neither of us cared enough to gamble and lose,
or was brave enough to risk and win.
So ended another sad chapter in our family's sad history.

BUDDY

Staff members knew Johnny was softhearted
for animals, especially those maltreated,
like the shepherd abandoned at
Germantown Hospital's main entrance.

Johnny refused involvement. Fellow workers
persisted. Wrapped later on in a blanket,
compassion brought Buddy home.
Water. Food. Stench of neglect ignored.

With care and observation—too sick,
best to put Buddy down, advised the vet.
Sad. Reluctant. Johnny consented.
Buddy's loss was felt for a long time.

STELLAR DESTINATION

Joe called, arrived home safely in Montrose.
We thanked each other again for gifts: pasta,
peaches, olive oil, capers, mango chutney—
mutual gifts mutually appreciated.

After Joe's call I felt sad, not so much
hearing of cousin Cecilia's or Tommy's old
friend, Tony Ruggieri's death, but
for our lives faster becoming emptier.

Faster emptying lives, surviving cousins
almost incommunicado. Over the years
our family's scandals honed into fables
sordid as the career of an L.A. porn star.

Stars were souls, the ancients believed.
Thousands of once noble and petty lives
glistened in celestial constellations.
Stellar destination, soul's infinity.

PHONE CALL

Phone's fancy ring disturbed quiet house,
caller ID identified: JOHN TACCONELLI,
my self-estranged younger brother.

"Hello." Pause. "Hello?" Another pause.
Each hello an invitation—response,
restrained emotion's shallow breathing.

Johnny's anonymity I respected. If I hang up,
I thought, he'd have time to gather himself,
call later. One last, "Hello?" Silence.

I hang up. Silence. I'm still waiting. Silence.

BLOOD OF ANCESTORS

HOLY CARD

1.

Tucked inside the birthday card
cousins Joe and Liz sent,
a saccharine holy card—plastic
laminated Saint Joseph cradling
in his arms the Child Jesus.

2.

They came one day, not
the elite Knights of Columbus,
but two smooth talking Masons
promising my father more business,
more money, success—if he joined.

Grease-stained hands opened ornate
National cash register, my father
pulled out a holy card, Saint Joseph,
patron saint of workers—held it
out and said, "This is my religion."

COUSIN ELIZABETH'S BURIAL

Misty rain softly saturated the stripped tarpaulin canopy above Liz's grave site—muddy soil neatly concealed under a green blanket of plastic grass.

Protecting ourselves from penetrating wetness, grieving mourners huddled beneath drooping canopy; our unspoken need to be close to family and friends surrounding sepulchered void waiting to hold Liz—till hosts of angels sounding golden trumpets fiercely loud come to awaken Liz from sleep. We will know then, finally and forever, what catechism taught, perhaps doubted, had indeed sustained us to that very moment's inevitability.

Holy water sprinkled, rite's consoling prayers concluded, to ease farewell's bitter harshness—lovingly we placed yellow, white, pink roses on blessed casket's shiny surface.

Afterwards we chatted. Some relatives had not seen each other for years. Once beautiful Italian peasant faces had grown old like faces from ancient tarnished coins, faces of austere Republican Romans who quit tilled fields to fight invading Gauls. Generations of proud heritage passed through hard centuries, endless genetic procession—blood thicker than water,

and Liz, too quickly gone, who generously gave love away—who, while giving birth to Lori, hemorrhaged, hovered near death, entered "a place of boundless light draped with curtains of light." Mother and daughter survived. Liz no longer feared death.

Parents, brothers, sisters, ancestors joyfully welcomed Liz to their glistening constellation—our heavenly family awaits us.

COUSIN MARY MARGARET

Lovely, her hands clasped, fingers intertwining
like a lieder singer in concert performing—
sincerity of gesture, spirit expansive,
twenty years her students into their future
has nurtured. Italian heart overflowing.

BIG JOE

for cousin Joe Virgilio

Big Joe is dead.
He lived life
by his rules,
hard to grasp,
and yet—it is
his yet I mourn.

COMARE MARY, COMPARE HENRY, AND JUNIOR

It was love I felt when we visited Comare Mary,
Compare Henry, and Junior on Morris,
a quiet side street in Wayne,
their ochre-colored stucco house;
    kitchen's spotless black and white tiled floor,
    always offered was a glass of ginger ale,
    and of course, anise sprinkled biscotti,
    most extraordinary was their library of books.

I was attracted to Junior's good looks, raspy
voice, pensive silence—to their friendliness.
I was used to abusive brothers who
lacked the Marini's heavenly cordiality.

After we left I would sink into a child's
solitary world submerged in a family
condemned to its inescapable insanities.

TWO COMARI MARYS

Fastidious carpenter, tools orderly
as his life—yet slowly Compare Henry
grew confused, behavior erratic.
Frantic when he drove off in the car,
not knowing if he'd return safely,
Comare Mary called Ma, her Comare Mary.

Two comari alone—Comare Mary's only
son, Junior, discharged from the Navy,
abandoned parents and America,
married and remained in far away Japan;
and Ma, isolated with in-laws,
lived miles from family in Poughkeepsie.

Late afternoon the phone rang.
Compare Henry disappeared.
I remember Ma's barely audible whispering,
the long silent pauses.
In each other two comari Marys found solace,
until husbands came home.

THE BLESSING

Sunday afternoon you and Ba returned,
having visited Compare Henry where
those who lost their minds were confined,
before they vanished into memory.

You were touched by the pitiful sight
—among rows of pallid patients seated
on stone benches—Compare Henry, lost
in a world without his carpenter's tools.

How I wished, you said, the Sacred Heart
would appear, hands upraised in blessing,
restoring health, healing wounded minds.

No Sacred Heart appeared, no blessing—
only your sacred heart's unspoken blessing,
bleeding for Compare Henry, and for us.

ALMOST MORNING

Almost morning, first birds calling, I'm half sleeping
dreaming of you, Comare Mary. Though you are dead
a long time, I decide to visit. Entering the driveway I see
no ochre-colored stucco, only yellow aluminum siding.
Is this the right house, small "MARINI" sign says yes.
Through the window, you are seated at kitchen table.
I knock. Hunched over a cane and very, very old your
disbelieving smile greets me. We share ginger ale, biscotti.
After our visit I leave, drive away, then turn back.
I want to stay longer, but sadly, I drive off.

You were abandoned when Compare Henry lost his mind,
institutionalized, died alone. Abandoned too, by Junior
in Japan, teaching English to Japan Airlines employees.
U. S. Navy offered freedom, provided what escape.
Does Junior think of you, or remember relatives in the
     States.
Fluent in new language, at ease with new customs,
     married
not an Italian, but a Japanese girl. Life equals change.
Nothing remains the same. Dream. Reality. No matter.
Life's legacy, irretrievable losses we learn to endure.

SECRET EPISODE

Every summer in my teens we visited my
mother's family for a week or two in Poughkeepsie,
stayed with Grandma at 188 Main Street.

Below her apartment, Uncle Tony's barber shop was
on one side, on the other, Uncle Jimmy's shoe repair
between them, Grandma's apartment door.

That night noisy relatives were not crowded around
kitchen table. No one was there. Bathed, wearing only
jockey shorts I lounged on the living room sofa.

The door opened. Someone climbed the stairs.
Pretending to be asleep, I felt Uncle Tony
leaning over me like a cobra ready to strike.

Suddenly, Uncle Tony's lips were close
enough he could steal an incestuous kiss.
What was he staring at. What was he thinking.

Heart pounding, my breathing barely controlled,
Uncle Tony stood up, descended the stairs quietly.
The door closed gently.

BLOOD OF ANCESTORS

Before heading home to Philadelphia after a weekend in Poughkeepsie, Johnny and I drove Aunt Virginia to Saint Peter's Cemetery to pay respects to Uncle Jimmy and other relatives.

Among granite tombstones, marble madonnas, angels, crosses Aunt Virginia led us to Uncle Jimmy's grave. Summer vacations in Poughkeepsie, Johnny and I remembered how Uncle Jimmy repaired our shoes— highly polished, they looked brand new.

Nearby were buried Joseph and Fanny Virgilio. Too young to remember Grandpa, I remembered dark circles surrounding Grandma's sad eyes, my headaches cured by *contra malocchio* prayers Grandma prayed over a dish of water and drops of oil.

Also nearby, Uncle Phil, who died in his thirties and youngest son, Peter, at five. As a joke, Uncle Phil hid dollar bills in thick waves of his black hair. Playing along the curb and cars parked on Main Street, Peter was struck by a careless driver in front of Uncle Tony's barber shop and Uncle Jimmy's shoe repair.

Aunt Connie and Uncle Joe arrived later. Every Sunday they visited Joseph's grave. Joseph's successful Manhattan hairstyling career ended tragically with AIDS. Devastated by the loss of their only son, Aunt Connie and Uncle Joe aged by decades.

Perfect October Sunday afternoon, red maples and burnished oaks scattered leaves everywhere. Drawn together to Saint Peter's Cemetery by blood of ancestors— Aunt Virginia, Aunt Connie, Uncle Joe, Johnny and I silently shared our grief.

I REMEMBER

I remember tedious three-hour drives in a crowded car,
Rt. 9 along the Hudson heading to Poughkeepsie
—anticipated summertime visits to my mother's
younger, passionate, boisterous family.

Above Uncle Tony's barber shop, and Uncle Jimmy's
shoe repair, Grandma Fanny Virgilio lived, their
shops between her apartment door. Widowed young
with five sons, two daughters—hard years encircled
Grandma's Mater Dolorosa eyes with dark shadows.
Around Grandma's kitchen table everyone found home.

Returning from the doctor's office for a flu shot,
Grandma climbed the stairs, sat down at kitchen
table, and died. Extinguished, the mother's
love that bound together those who became
only closer, more possessive, more protective.

Today, Little Joe from Florida called, sad news,
Aunt "G" died, Ma's younger sister, who so much
loved my mother. I can still see them laughing
together shopping for bargains on Main Street.
Last of the old order, Aunt Virginia was dead.
Estranged as I had become I felt profound loss.

Florida, North Carolina, California, Pennsylvania,
Connecticut, and of course, Poughkeepsie. What
keeps us remaining distant cousins in touch—far
flung stars, universe gradually disintegrating.

GAINS AND LOSSES

OUR PORCH

My bruises are breadcrumbs — trace the way.
   —Janet Mason

1.

Along the side of our porch, I remember red ramblers
Ba planted. I remember the rose-wreathed
trellis arching over the swinging latticed gate,
the concrete steps Ba made, three slender white
wooden Tuscan columns supporting the porch's roof,
its ceiling painted pale sky blue, the low brick
wall on which those columns rested with Ma's
bright pots of house plants neatly in a row,
and the hedge always meticulously trimmed short.
Today, the porch is asphalt and parked cars.

2.

Early summer evening, I sat watching traffic passing
while Nonna prayed her rosary. As if on a mission
earnest young people sped by. Of course, it was
Saturday night, guys and girls on dates went to
the movies, or friends met other friends—
I suffocated with adolescent loneliness. Suddenly,
like spontaneous combustion, I burst into tears.
"C'a successe, c'a successe?" "What's happened?"
Pleaded Nonna. "Ninte," "Nothing," I cried,
got up and went inside. The rest I've forgotten.

3.

Much of the past has been erased, displaced by a
present in which I rejoice at my cohesive sense of
identity, but in my memory, to the porch of the place
where I grew up, with its blue, white, and orange
aluminum and wicker lawn chairs, I still return.

GAINS AND LOSSES

Romantic scene like a Hollywood movie—
Cape May beach wedding with handsome,
loving young couple surrounded by smiling
family and well-wishing friends.

No church wedding. Muffling wind muted
civil ceremony's legally binding words.
Later, no baptisms—later still, children's gifts
will celebrate Christmas without Christ Child.

Visiting these dear friends, I sense sometimes
profound feelings of existential emptiness.
I ponder what's been lost along the way,
wonder what, if anything, has been gained.

NOT OFTEN

Not often, not even rarely
—backyard of the new,
old house we bought in sixty-six
on Pennsylvania Avenue,
every spring its blue surprise,
hundreds of Siberian Squills—
I saw inching among dry leaves,
clumps of wild onions and garlic,
a large dark brown turtle, alone
in its crenellated carapace,
heading towards the Barones.
How long had the turtle lived in
the backyard. Forty-four years since,
I wonder if on warm mornings,
or cool late afternoons,
the turtle still searches, still finds.

WINE CELLAR

In the cellar's small anteroom,
concrete walls whitewashed,
nothing remains—five
empty oak barrels smashed,
their rusty iron hoops crushed,
trash removed by new owners—
forty years to emptiness.

If you pause long enough,
concentrate hard enough,
faintest fragrance still lingers,
still heard, gurgling sounds of
newly pressed grapes fermenting.
Gone now the wine makers,
slowly becoming more forgotten.

ALBERT TACCONELLI holds a B. F. A. from Philadelphia College of Art in Illustration, and M. S. from Chestnut Hill College in Counseling Psychology. Serving in the US Army, Tacconelli art directed Fort Bragg's *J. F. Kennedy Museum For Special Warfare.*

Former graphic arts designer, Tacconelli devotes time to art, and to poetry which has appeared in journals: *Paterson Literary Review, Philadelphia Poets, Endicott Review, Mad Poets Review, VIA,* and in several anthologies: *Avanti Popolo: Italian-Americans Writers Sailing Beyond Columbus, Fourteenth Poetry Ink Anniversary Anthology,* American Italian Historical Association: *Italian Americans and the Arts & Culture,* American Italian Historical Association: *We've Always Been Here,* The American Voice in Poetry: *Legacy of Whitman, Williams, and Ginsberg,* Remembrances, and Humorous Happenings While Traveling in Italy.

Tacconelli has presented work at Hofstra University, John D. Calandra Italian American Institute, Free Library of Philadelphia and the Fumo Family Branch, Passaic County Community College's *Crossing Boundaries: Visual Art by Writers,* Churchill's Cafe, Cornelia Street Cafe, Robin's Bookstore, Giovanni's Room, and Libretto Book Club.

Tacconelli won Honorable Mention in *Ohio Poetry Association's Summer Solstice Contest,* runner up in *Philadelphia Poets First Annual John And Rose Petracca & Family Award,* and received both the *Allen Ginsberg Poetry Contest* Editor's Choice and Honorable Mention.

Current chapbooks include: *Two Countries One Heart, The Laurenzi Poems, Short Stack, That One Pure Time.*

The Philadelphia Sketch Club, Mariani Italian American Museum and Institute, Galleria Artemisia, Passaic County Community College have exhibited Tacconelli's art. Several of Tacconelli's paintings and prints are included in the permanent collection of contemporary art at Passaic County Community College.

VIA FOLIOS
A refereed book series dedicated to the culture of Italians and Italian Americans.

RACHEL GUIDO DEVRIES. *A Woman Unknown in Her Bones.* Vol. 105, Poetry. $11
BERNARD BRUNO. *A Tear and A Tear in My Heart.* Vol. 104, Memoir. $20
FELIX STEFANILE. *Songs of the Sparrow.* Vol. 103, Poetry. $30
FRANK POLIZZI. *A New Life with Bianca.* Vol. 102, Poetry. $10
GIL FAGIANI. *Stone Walls.* Vol. 101, Poetry. $14
LOUISE DESALVO. *Casting Off.* Vol. 100, Fiction. $22
MARY JO BONA. *I stop waiting for You.* Vol. 99, Poetry. $12
RACHEL GUIDO DEVRIES. *Stati zitta, Josie.* Vol. 98, Children's Literature. $8
GRACE CAVALIERI. *The Mandate of Heaven.* Vol. 97, Poetry. $11
MARISA FRASCA. *Via incanto.* Vol. 96, Poetry. $12
DOUGLAS GLADSTONE. *Carving a Niche for Himself.* Vol. 95, History. $12
MARIA TERRONE. *Eye to Eye.* Vol. 94, Poetry. $14
CONSTANCE SANCETTA. *Here in Cerchio* Vol. 93, Local History. $15
MARIA MAZZIOTTI GILLAN. *Ancestors' Song* Vol. 92, Poetry. $14
DARRELL FUSARO. *What if Godzilla Just Wanted a Hug?* Essays.
MICHAEL PARENTI. *Waiting for Yesterday: Pages from a Street Kid's Life.* Vol. 90,
    Memoir. $15
ANNIE LANZILOTTO, *Schistsong,* Vol. 89, Poetry, $15
EMANUEL DI PASQUALE, *Love Lines,* Vol. 88, Poetry, $10
CAROSONE & LOGIUDICE. *Our Naked Lives.* Vol. 87, Essays. $15
JAMES PERICONI. *Strangers in a Strange Land: A Survey of Italian-Language American
    Books.* Vol. 86, Book History. $24
DANIELA GIOSEFFI, *Escaping La Vita Della Cucina,* Vol. 85, Essays & Creative
    Writing. $22
MARIA FAMÀ, *Mystics in the Family,* Vol. 84, Poetry, $10
ROSSANA DEL ZIO, *From Bread and Tomatoes to Zuppa di Pesce "Ciambotto."* Vol. 83,
    $15
LORENZO DELBOCA, *Polentoni,* Vol. 82, Italian Studies, $15
SAMUEL GHELLI, *A Reference Grammar,* Vol. 81, Italian Language. $36
ROSS TALARICO, *Sled Run,* Vol. 80, Fiction. $15
FRED MISURELLA, *Only Sons,* Vol. 79, Fiction. $14
FRANK LENTRICCHIA, *The Portable Lentricchia,* Vol. 78, Fiction. $16
RICHARD VETERE, *The Other Colors in a Snow Storm,* Vol. 77, Poetry. $10
GARIBALDI LAPOLLA, *Fire in the Flesh,* Vol. 76, Fiction & Criticism. $25
GEORGE GUIDA, *The Pope Stories,* Vol. 75, Prose. $15
ROBERT VISCUSI, *Ellis Island,* Vol. 74, Poetry. $28
ELENA GIANINI BELOTTI, *The Bitter Taste of Strangers Bread,* Vol. 73, Fiction, $24
PINO APRILE, *Terroni,* Vol. 72, Italian Studies, $20
EMANUEL DI PASQUALE, *Harvest,* Vol. 71, Poetry, $10
ROBERT ZWEIG, *Return to Naples,* Vol. 70, Memoir, $16
AIROS & CAPPELLI, *Guido,* Vol. 69, Italian/American Studies, $12
FRED GARDAPHÉ, *Moustache Pete is Dead! Long Live Moustache Pete!,* Vol. 67,
    Literature/Oral History, $12
PAOLO RUFFILLI, *Dark Room/Camera oscura,* Vol. 66, Poetry, $11
HELEN BAROLINI, *Crossing the Alps,* Vol. 65, Fiction, $14
COSMO FERRARA, *Profiles of Italian Americans,* Vol. 64, Italian Americana, $16
GIL FAGIANI, *Chianti in Connecticut,* Vol. 63, Poetry, $10

BASSETTI & D'ACQUINO, *Italic Lessons*, Vol. 62, Italian/American Studies, $10

CAVALIERI & PASCARELLI, Eds., *The Poet's Cookbook*, Vol. 61, Poetry/Recipes, $12

EMANUEL DI PASQUALE, *Siciliana*, Vol. 60, Poetry, $8

NATALIA COSTA, Ed., *Bufalini*, Vol. 59, Poetry. $18.

RICHARD VETERE, *Baroque*, Vol. 58, Fiction. $18.

LEWIS TURCO, *La Famiglia/The Family*, Vol. 57, Memoir, $15

NICK JAMES MILETI, *The Unscrupulous*, Vol. 56, Humanities, $20

BASSETTI, ACCOLLA, D'AQUINO, *Italici: An Encounter with Piero Bassetti*, Vol. 55, Italian Studies, $8

GIOSE RIMANELLI, *The Three-legged One*, Vol. 54, Fiction, $15

CHARLES KLOPP, *Bele Antiche Stòrie*, Vol. 53, Criticism, $25

JOSEPH RICAPITO, *Second Wave*, Vol. 52, Poetry, $12

GARY MORMINO, *Italians in Florida*, Vol. 51, History, $15

GIANFRANCO ANGELUCCI, *Federico F.*, Vol. 50, Fiction, $15

ANTHONY VALERIO, *The Little Sailor*, Vol. 49, Memoir, $9

ROSS TALARICO, *The Reptilian Interludes*, Vol. 48, Poetry, $15

RACHEL GUIDO DE VRIES, *Teeny Tiny Tino's Fishing Story*, Vol. 47, Children's Literature, $6

EMANUEL DI PASQUALE, *Writing Anew*, Vol. 46, Poetry, $15

MARIA FAMÀ, *Looking For Cover*, Vol. 45, Poetry, $12

ANTHONY VALERIO, *Toni Cade Bambara's One Sicilian Night*, Vol. 44, Poetry, $10

EMANUEL CARNEVALI, Dennis Barone, Ed., *Furnished Rooms*, Vol. 43, Poetry, $14

BRENT ADKINS, et al., Ed., *Shifting Borders, Negotiating Places*, Vol. 42, Proceedings, $18

GEORGE GUIDA, *Low Italian*, Vol. 41, Poetry, $11

GARDAPHÈ, GIORDANO, TAMBURRI, *Introducing Italian Americana*, Vol. 40, Italian/American Studies, $10

DANIELA GIOSEFFI, *Blood Autumn/Autunno di sangue*, Vol. 39, Poetry, $15/$25

FRED MISURELLA, *Lies to Live by*, Vol. 38, Stories, $15

STEVEN BELLUSCIO, *Constructing a Bibliography*, Vol. 37, Italian Americana, $15

ANTHONY JULIAN TAMBURRI, Ed., *Italian Cultural Studies 2002*, Vol. 36, Essays, $18

BEA TUSIANI, *con amore*, Vol. 35, Memoir, $19

FLAVIA BRIZIO-SKOV, Ed., *Reconstructing Societies in the Aftermath of War*, Vol. 34, History, $30

TAMBURRI, et al., Eds., *Italian Cultural Studies 2001*, Vol. 33, Essays, $18

ELIZABETH G. MESSINA, Ed., *In Our Own Voices*, Vol. 32, Italian/American Studies, $25

STANISLAO G. PUGLIESE, *Desperate Inscriptions*, Vol. 31, History, $12

HOSTERT & TAMBURRI, Eds., *Screening Ethnicity*, Vol. 30, Italian/American Culture, $25

G. PARATI & B. LAWTON, Eds., *Italian Cultural Studies*, Vol. 29, Essays, $18

HELEN BAROLINI, *More Italian Hours*, Vol. 28, Fiction, $16

FRANCO NASI, Ed., *Intorno alla Via Emilia*, Vol. 27, Culture, $16

ARTHUR L. CLEMENTS, *The Book of Madness & Love*, Vol. 26, Poetry, $10

JOHN CASEY, et al., *Imagining Humanity*, Vol. 25, Interdisciplinary Studies, $18

ROBERT LIMA, *Sardinia/Sardegna*, Vol. 24, Poetry, $10

DANIELA GIOSEFFI, *Going On*, Vol. 23, Poetry, $10

ROSS TALARICO, *The Journey Home*, Vol. 22, Poetry, $12

EMANUEL DI PASQUALE, *The Silver Lake Love Poems*, Vol. 21, Poetry, $7

JOSEPH TUSIANI, *Ethnicity*, Vol. 20, Poetry, $12

www.ingramcontent.com/pod-product-compliance
Lightning Source LLC
La Vergne TN
LVHW051604080426
835510LV00020B/3120